CONTINENTS UNCOVERED

AUSTRALIA AND ANTARCTICA

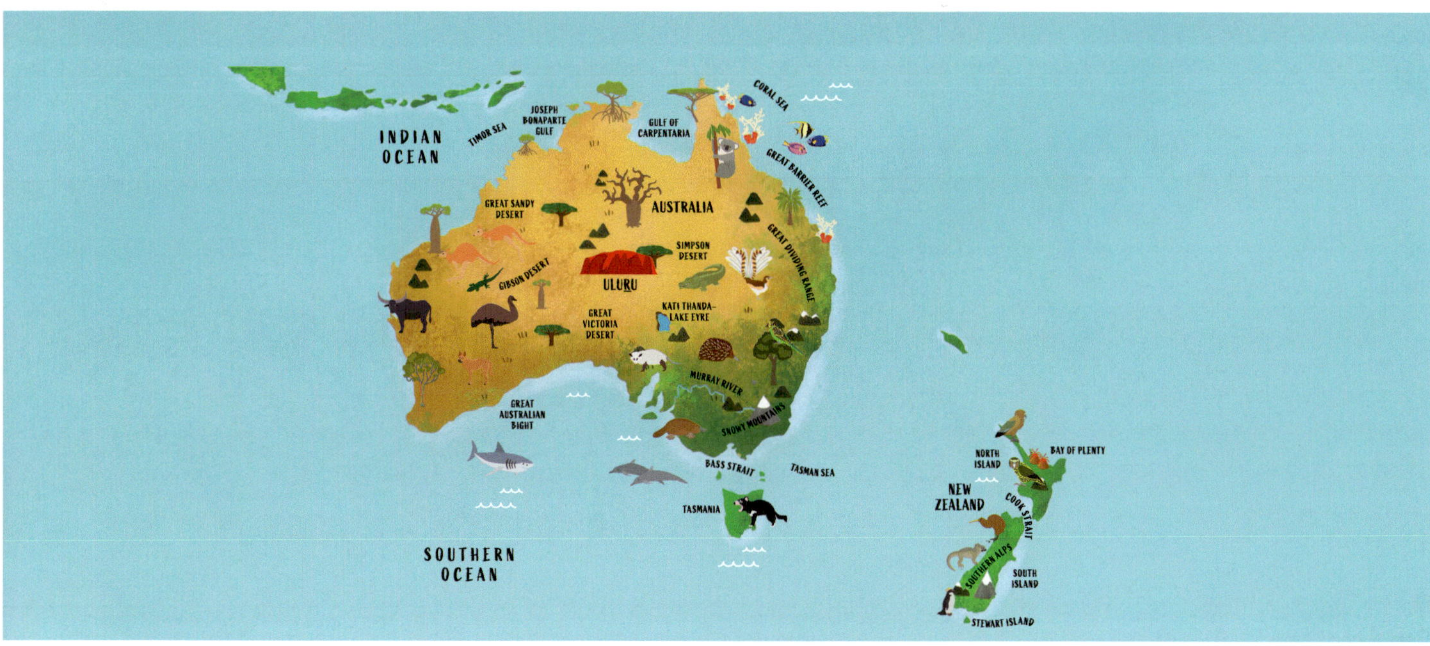

Written by Rob Colson
Illustrated by Josy Bloggs

Enslow PUBLISHING

Published in 2025 by Enslow Publishing, LLC
2544 Clinton Street
Buffalo, NY 14224

First published in Great Britain in 2023 by Hodder & Stoughton

Series Editor: Amy Pimperton
Series Designer: Ed Simkins
Illustrator: Josy Bloggs
Map illustrator: Amy Zhing

Manufactured in the United States of America

CPSIA compliance information: Batch #CSENS25: For further information contact Enslow Publishing LLC, New York, New York at 1-800-398-2504.

Please visit our website, www.enslowpublishing.com. For a free color catalog of all our high-quality books, call toll free 1-800-398-2504 or fax 1-877-980-4454.

Cataloging-in-Publication Data

Names: Colson, Rob, author. | Bloggs, Josy, illustrator.
Title: Australia and Antarctica / by Rob Colson, illustrated by Josy Bloggs.
Description: Buffalo, NY : Enslow Publishing, 2025. | Series: Continents uncovered | Includes glossary and index.
Identifiers: ISBN 9781978539105 (pbk.) | ISBN 9781978539112 (library bound) | ISBN 9781978539129 (ebook)
Subjects: LCSH: Oceania--Juvenile literature.
Classification: LCC DU17.C657 2025 | DDC 995--dc2

We recommend adult supervision at all times while doing the activities in this book. Always be aware that craft materials may contain allergens, so check the packaging for allergens if there is a risk of an allergic reaction. Anyone with a known allergy must avoid these.

- Wear an apron and cover surfaces.
- Tie back long hair.
- Ask an adult for help with cutting and glueing.
- Check materials for allergens.

CONTENTS

WHERE IN THE WORLD?

Located in the Southern Hemisphere, Oceania is the smallest continent by land mass. Most of the land is found on Australia, which is classed as a continent rather than an island. New Zealand covers two large islands, while the island of New Guinea is shared by two countries: Indonesia and Papua New Guinea. Thousands of smaller islands spread across the Pacific Ocean. The huge continent of Antarctica is located around the South Pole.

POLITICAL MAP

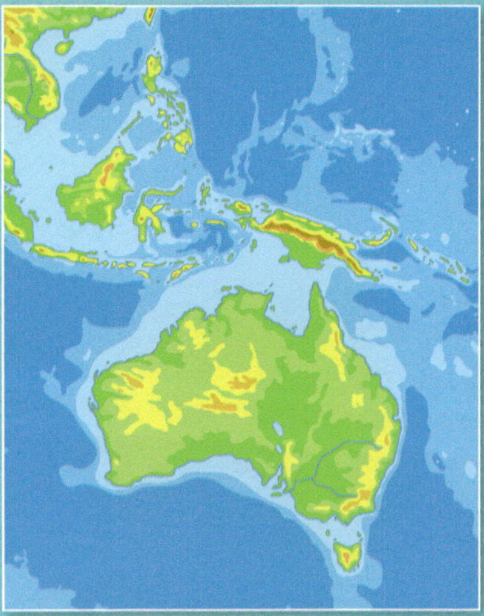

PHYSICAL MAP

MAKING MAPS

Mapmakers create maps that show different types of information. Political maps, such as the map at far left, show features like countries. Physical maps, like the map to the left, show geographical features like altitude. In the physical map, the higher ground is colored brown and yellow and the low ground is colored green.

HABITATS

A habitat is an area that is home to a particular group of plants and animals. The habitats of Oceania range from the lush rainforest of New Guinea (1) to the baking hot deserts of the Australian outback (2). Off the eastern coast of Australia stretches the Great Barrier Reef (3), which is home to a diverse range of sea creatures. Very few plants or animals can endure the extreme cold of the Antarctic Peninsula (4), where the largest plants grow only a couple of inches tall.

FACTS

- Area (Oceania): 3.28 million square miles (8.5 million square kilometers)
- Major rivers: Sepik River (Papua New Guinea), Murray River (Australia), Waikato River (New Zealand)
- Highest peak: Mount Vinson (Antarctica), 16,050 feet (4,892 meters)
- Major mountain ranges: New Guinea Highlands (New Guinea), Great Dividing Range (Australia), Southern Alps (New Zealand)

NEW GUINEA
PUNCAK JAYA
BISMARCK SEA
SOLOMON SEA
TORRES STRAIT
CORAL SEA
JOSEPH BONAPARTE GULF
TIMOR SEA
INDIAN OCEAN
GULF OF CARPENTARIA
GREAT BARRIER REEF
GREAT SANDY DESERT
AUSTRALIA
SIMPSON DESERT
GREAT DIVIDING RANGE
GIBSON DESERT
ULURU
KATI THANDA-LAKE EYRE
GREAT VICTORIA DESERT
MURRAY RIVER
GREAT AUSTRALIAN BIGHT
SNOWY MOUNTAINS
BASS STRAIT
TASMAN SEA
TASMANIA
SOUTHERN OCEAN
N
W
E
S

OCEANIA

Oceania is home to many plants and animals found nowhere else on Earth, including mammals like kangaroos, wallabies, and koalas. On the continent of Australia, there are many species of deadly spiders and snakes. The islands of New Zealand and New Guinea have different wildlife than Australia. Lacking native mammals other than bats and some marine mammals, New Zealand has a wide range of unique bird species.

MARSUPIALS

Many species of marsupial are found in Oceania. Marsupials give birth to tiny young, which develop inside their mother's pouch. Oceania is isolated from the rest of the world geographically, which has allowed marsupials to evolve into many different forms. The shy sugar glider is a small squirrel-like creature that glides from tree to tree feeding on nectar.

ULURU

Uluru is a huge chunk of sandstone that stands 1,142 feet (348 m) above the flat desert landscape below. Uluru is at the center of Uluru-Kata Tjuta National Park. The park contains natural springs, waterholes, and caves and is home to many animals, including red kangaroos, emus, frogs, and bats.

BUSHFIRES

During dry periods in Australia, many areas suffer from bushfires. The fires can sweep quickly through forests, killing animals that cannot outrun them. While bushfires have a devastating effect in the short term, the forests are able to recover. Eucalyptus trees are adapted to deal with bushfires. Their seeds are protected from the flames by woody capsules called gumnuts. After the fire has passed, the gumnuts open up to release the seeds into the ash and they start growing into new trees.

NEW GUINEA RAINFOREST

Sitting just south of the equator, the island of New Guinea is covered in one of the world's largest tropical rainforests. More than 13,000 species of plants are found on New Guinea, more than on any other island. It is also home to hundreds of colorful bird species.

FACTS

- The echidna is a mammal that lays eggs. It has powerful limbs and sharp claws, which it uses to dig up ants and termites. Its body is covered in sharp quills to protect it from predators.

- The cassowary is a large bird that lives deep in the forest. It cannot fly, but it can run at up to 31 miles (50 km) per hour and is a strong swimmer.

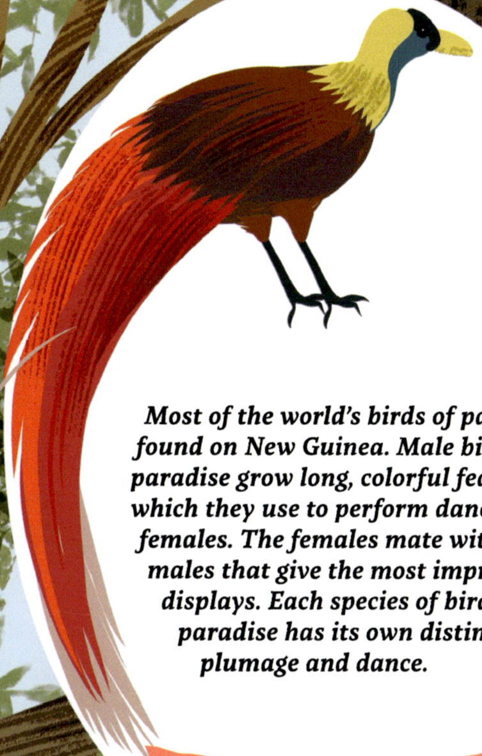

Most of the world's birds of paradise are found on New Guinea. Male birds of paradise grow long, colorful feathers, which they use to perform dances for females. The females mate with the males that give the most impressive displays. Each species of bird of paradise has its own distinctive plumage and dance.

BIRDS OF PARADISE

ORCHID

BANDICOOT

ACTIVITY

Seeing bubbles

Trees are vital to life on our planet. Their leaves produce oxygen in a process called photosynthesis. Watch how bubbles of oxygen form when you submerge a leaf in a bowl of water.

1. Collect two or three large green leaves. With an adult's help, place the leaves in a shallow tray and weigh them down by placing a small rock on each one. Pour enough water over the leaves to completely cover them.

2. Leave the tray in a place with direct sunlight for one hour. When you come back, can you see tiny bubbles around the leaves? This is the oxygen they have made.

3. For comparison, repeat the experiment but leave the tray in a dark place for an hour. When you return, there will be no bubbles. This is because the leaves need sunlight to make oxygen.

GREAT BARRIER REEF

The Great Barrier Reef is the world's largest coral reef system, extending for more than 1,430 miles (2,300 km) off the coast of Queensland, Australia. It contains around 3,000 separate reefs and more than 600 islands. More than 1,500 species of fish and 4,000 species of mollusks make their home among the colorful corals.

FACTS

- The dugong, or sea cow, is a large mammal that swims gently through the shallow seas around the reefs, grazing on sea grass.

- The blanket octopus takes its name from the long, fleshy cape between the arms of the females. The females grow up to 6.5 feet (2 m) in length, but the males measure just 1 inch (2.5 cm) — smaller than a walnut!

CORAL

A coral reef is covered by millions of tiny creatures called polyps. The polyps catch food from the water with their tentacle-like arms. They are attached to the surface of the reef by a hard limestone skeleton. When the polyps die, their skeletons remain, slowly building up the reef structure. The tiny algae that live inside the polyps create the bright colors of the reef.

ACTIVITY

Octopus

Make a paper plate octopus. Ask an adult for help when using scissors and the hole punch.

1. Cut a paper plate in half and paint one side with blue paint. Allow the paint to dry.

2. Use a hole punch to punch eight evenly spaced holes along the straight side of the plate.

3. Cut eight strands of colored yarn about 12 inches (30 cm) long. Feed one strand through each hole in the plate from the front and tie a knot at the back.

4. Add googly eyes to complete your octopus.

AUSTRALIAN OUTBACK

Away from the coasts, most of the interior of Australia is dry. In addition to the red desert, there are regions of scrubland and grassy woodland. Much of the continent's unique wildlife makes its home in the outback, well adapted to the harsh environment.

FACTS

- The red kangaroo is the largest mammal native to Australia. It can hop huge distances. A large male can cover up to 30 feet (9 m) in one leap, reaching a height of 10 feet (3 m) along the way.

- The soil in the Australian outback appears to be red due to its high iron content. As the iron begins to rust, it turns red and breaks apart into sand.

THORNY DEVIL

The thorny devil is a lizard that lives in central Australia. It is covered in sharp spines for protection and has a false head on its back, which it uses to confuse predators. To survive, the thorny devil collects dew on its skin in the early morning. The dew is channeled to its mouth along grooves between the spines. It can also absorb water from damp sand through its skin.

ACTIVITY

Walking water

The thorny devil absorbs water through its skin by a process called capillary action. Watch how capillary action moves liquids in this walking water experiment.

1. Place three clear plastic cups in a row and fill the first and third cups with water. With adult supervision, add two drops of red food coloring to the first cup and two drops of blue food coloring to the third cup. Leave the middle cup empty.

2. Fold a paper towel in half. Hang one side of the paper towel in the red cup and drape the other side into the middle cup. Do the same with another paper towel, from the blue cup into the middle cup.

3. Watch how the water travels along the paper towels and into the empty cup. The water from the first and third cups will mix together in the middle cup. What color water do they make in the middle cup?

TONGARIRO NATIONAL PARK

Located in the center of New Zealand's North Island, Tongariro National Park covers an area around three active volcanoes. On the lower slopes of the snow-capped volcanoes are scrublands and forests with streams, lakes, and spectacular waterfalls. Some of New Zealand's rarest animals are found in the park, including the North Island brown kiwi and New Zealand's only falcon.

FACTS

- Many mammals have been introduced to New Zealand by humans, but the only native land mammals are two species of bat — the short-tailed bat and the long-tailed bat, both of which are found in the park.
- According to Māori legend, the priest Ngātoroirangi climbed the volcano Mount Tongariro and claimed for his people all the land that he could see from the summit.

KIWI

The kiwi is a flightless bird that hunts at night. It has poor eyesight and sniffs out prey, such as insects and worms, using nostrils at the end of its long beak. Each year, a female kiwi lays one huge egg. While a kiwi is about the same size as a chicken, its eggs are six times larger than chicken eggs! Found only in New Zealand, the kiwi has become a national symbol for the country.

KAKA

BLUE DUCK

ACTIVITY

Tough eggs

Eggs are easily broken when you drop them. However, their oval shape makes them surprisingly strong so that they don't get crushed by the nesting parents. With an adult's help, test out the strength of chicken eggs with this simple experiment.

1. You will need three eggs and six plastic bottle caps of the same size. Place a bottle cap at either end of each egg and arrange the eggs in a triangle with a book on top, as shown.

2. Now add more books to the pile. How many books can your eggs hold without breaking? You may be surprised how high the pile can go! This is because an egg's oval shape distributes the weight evenly around the egg.

SOUTHERN ALPS

The Southern Alps, or Kā Tiritiri o te Moana, are a mountain range that stretches along most of the length of New Zealand's South Island. The peaks of the mountains are permanently covered in snow, but the lower slopes give way to beech forests, which are home to a wide variety of plants and animals.

FACTS

- Aoraki (Mount Cook) is the tallest mountain in New Zealand at 12,218 feet (3,724 m).

- With a body length of up to 4 inches (10 cm), the giant weta is one of the largest insects in the world. This flightless insect can be found at heights of up to 11,810 feet (3,600 m).

KEA

The kea is the only parrot in the world that lives in mountains. Kea are highly intelligent and curious birds. They live in groups and often work together to find food. Kea have been called the "clever clowns of the mountains" by scientists researching their intelligence. They often approach tourists and investigate their belongings, flying off with any small item that captures their interest.

ACTIVITY

Testing beaks

Beaks are like tools that birds use to find food. The kea has a long, curved beak, which it uses to dig for grubs. Experiment with different tools to see which shape is best to pick up different food items.

1. Ask an adult to help you lay out different food items on separate plates on the table. Make sure they are different shapes and hardness. You could use crackers, sunflower seeds, raisins, and soft candy, like gummy worms.

2. Select a variety of tools to test, such as a small spoon, tweezers, a toothpick, and a pair of chopsticks. Using only one hand, try to pick up just one of each food item and place it on an empty plate. Which tools are best for each food item?

THE PACIFIC ISLANDS

There are more than 25,000 islands scattered across the vast Pacific Ocean. Some of the islands were formed by volcanic eruptions, while others are coral reefs that have risen above sea level. Large animals are mostly absent from the islands, but many species of birds thrive in the South Pacific, safe from predators.

HAWAII

Hawaii, part of the United States, is an archipelago of 137 islands in the Pacific. The islands formed from a series of volcanic eruptions. The mighty volcano Mauna Loa covers half of the land mass of the island of Hawaii, the largest of the islands. It is an active volcano and has erupted more than 30 times since records were started in 1843.

COCONUTS

Coconut trees are found throughout the Pacific. Coconuts are light and their hard shells are water-resistant, which means that they can spread from island to island by drifting across the sea. Most scientists believe that the first coconut trees were brought to the South Pacific by early human settlers. They were a valuable source of food and water on long voyages as they remain edible for many months.

PACIFIC ATOLLS

An atoll is a ring-shaped coral reef rising above the water, creating an island rim enclosing an inner lagoon. Most of the world's atolls are found in the Pacific Ocean. The largest is Kiritimati, or Christmas Island, which has a perimeter of 93 miles (150 km). Few animals live there permanently, but seabirds nest on the island, which has the world's largest breeding colonies of the sooty tern, the phoenix petrel, and the Christmas shearwater.

FACTS

- The grey-green fruit dove is found only on Tahiti and nearby Moorea Island. It is hard to spot in the trees as its light green body and dark green wings blend in perfectly with the leaves.

- Many fruit trees have been introduced to Tahiti by humans. These include breadfruit, mangoes, avocados, and bananas.

TAHITI

Tahiti is the largest island in French Polynesia. The island formed from volcanic eruptions about 1 million years ago. Today, the hillsides of the steep volcanic mountains are covered in lush rainforest. The forests of French Polynesia are home to more than 90 species of birds. No mammals are native to the islands, but rats were brought there on ships from Europe. The rats threaten the native birds by stealing their eggs and attacking their young.

NATIONAL FLOWER

Despite its name, the Tahitian gardenia originates in Melanesia in the western Pacific. It was brought to Tahiti by early human settlers. This tropical shrub thrives on the island's steep volcanic hillsides. It produces white, wheel-shaped flowers. The people of Polynesia traditionally make flower necklaces and crowns from Tahitian gardenia. The flowers are also highly valued for their strong perfume and their medicinal properties.

ACTIVITY

Flower crown

Polynesians make crowns and necklaces from native flowers. With adult permission, make a crown from flowers that grow in your area. This one is made from dandelions.

1. Pick a bunch of dandelions with their stems intact. Trim the stems so that they are about 3 inches (8 cm) long.

2. Create a chain of dandelions by linking them together. Use your fingernail to make a hole in the middle of one dandelion stem and slip a second stem through it. Now make a hole in the middle of the second stem and slip a third through it.

3. Make a chain that is long enough to fit around your head, then link the ends of the chain together. With an adult's help, use scissors to trim any stems that stick out.

PEOPLE AND PLACES

The continent of Australia is Oceania's biggest country by population. To the north of Australia, New Guinea is home to an extremely diverse population. The islands of New Zealand to the southeast of the continent are the other major population center.

AUSTRALIA

The country of Australia occupies the Australian continent and the island of Tasmania. Most of the population lives in the major cities around the coast. About 600,000 people are First Nations Australians — descendants of the first people to arrive there 50,000 years ago. Settlers from Europe began arriving more than 230 years ago. More recently, many people from Asia have settled in Australia.

AUSTRALIA

AREA: 2.97 MILLION SQUARE MILES (7.7 MILLION SQ KM)

POPULATION: 26 MILLION

MAIN LANGUAGE: ENGLISH

CAPITAL CITY: CANBERRA

NEW GUINEA

New Guinea is the world's second-largest island, after Greenland. It is split between two countries. The western half is part of Indonesia, while the eastern half is the independent country Papua New Guinea. Papua New Guinea is one of the most culturally diverse places on Earth. More than 850 different languages are spoken by the country's 8 million people. Many of its people choose to follow traditional ways of life with little influence from the modern world.

NEW ZEALAND

The islands of New Zealand were first populated by Polynesians about 800 years ago. Today, the descendants of the original settlers, known as Māori, make up about 20 percent of the population of 5 million. The Māori name for the country is Aotearoa. The majority of the population are of European descent, but Māori culture forms an important part of the country's identity. Before the start of an international game, many of New Zealand's sports teams perform the *haka*, a Māori ceremonial dance.

PEOPLE AND PLACES

Humans first arrived on the Pacific Islands around 30,000 years ago. By 1,000 years ago, nearly every island had been reached. There are three main cultural areas in the Pacific: Micronesia, Melanesia, and Polynesia. The remote islands of Polynesia were the last to be settled.

FIJI

AREA: 6,950 SQUARE MILES (18,000 SQ KM)

POPULATION: 920,000

MAIN LANGUAGES: FIJIAN, ENGLISH, FIJI HINDI

CAPITAL CITY: SUVA

FIJI

Fiji is a country in Melanesia made up of more than 330 volcanic islands, of which 110 are inhabited. Most of the country's 920,000 inhabitants live on the two main islands, Viti Levu and Vanua Levu. The islands were first settled by humans more than 3,000 years ago. Some Fijians follow the Hindu religion. Each year, the whole country comes together to celebrate the Hindu festival Diwali.

Honolulu HAWAII

EASTER ISLAND

More than 1,242 miles (2,000 km) from any other populated island, Easter Island is one of the most remote inhabited places in the world. Nearly 1,000 stone statues are placed around the island, looking inward. Called *moai*, these mysterious statues are several feet tall and weigh up to 88 tons. They were carved more than 500 years ago by the island's original inhabitants, the Rapa Nui, who arrived there in about 1200 CE. The moai are believed to represent the spirits of ancient ancestors.

RIBATI

MARQUESAS ISLANDS

EASTER ISLAND

POLYNESIA

PACIFIC OCEAN

BORA-BORA

PITCAIRN ISLAND

FRENCH POLYNESIA

TAHITI

COOK ISLANDS

SOCIETY ISLANDS

RUGBY NATIONS

Rugby union is a popular sport on many of the islands of the Pacific. New Zealand's All Blacks are the most successful rugby team in the world, and Fiji, Tonga, and Samoa all have strong teams. Fiji has enjoyed particular success in rugby sevens, a fast and dynamic form of the game featuring teams of 7 players rather than the 15 players in a full rugby match.

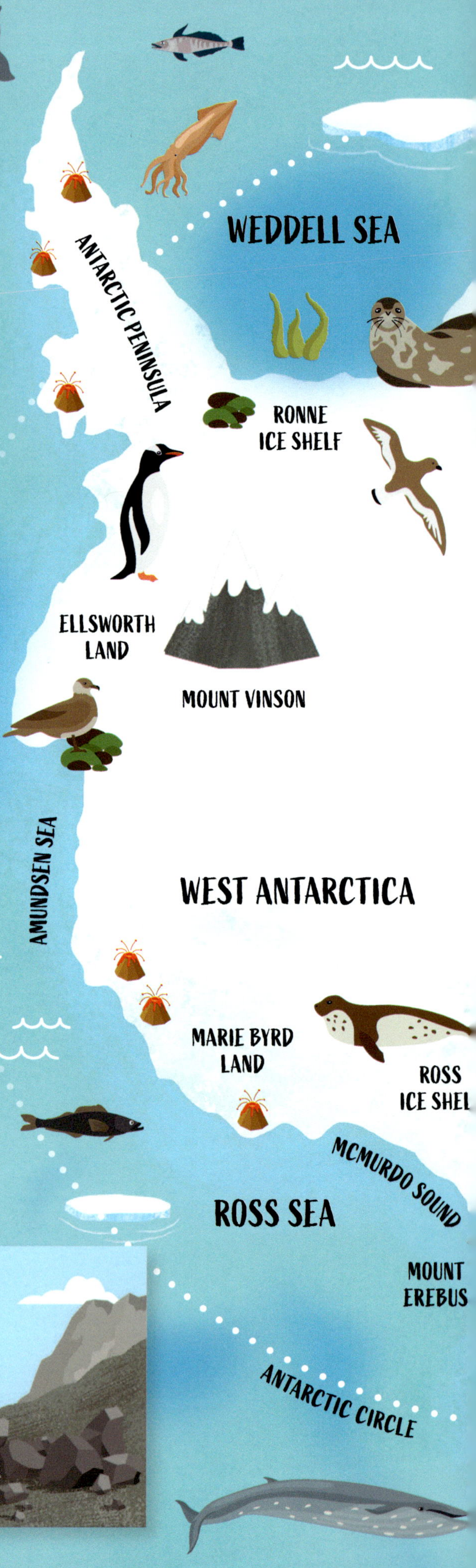

ANTARCTICA

The continent of Antarctica sits on top of the South Pole. The temperature never reaches above freezing point, so the snow that does fall never melts! Over thousands of years, the snow turns to ice. More than 90 percent of the world's ice is found on Antarctica. The continent is surrounded by a vast ice sheet, which reaches far over the Southern Ocean.

McMURDO DRY VALLEYS

The McMurdo Dry Valleys are a row of rocky snow-free valleys. This is one of the driest places in the world, battered by winds that can reach up to 200 miles (320 km) per hour. Space scientists test out equipment in the Dry Valleys, which are the closest place on Earth to the conditions on the surface of the planet Mars.

SOUTHERN OCEAN

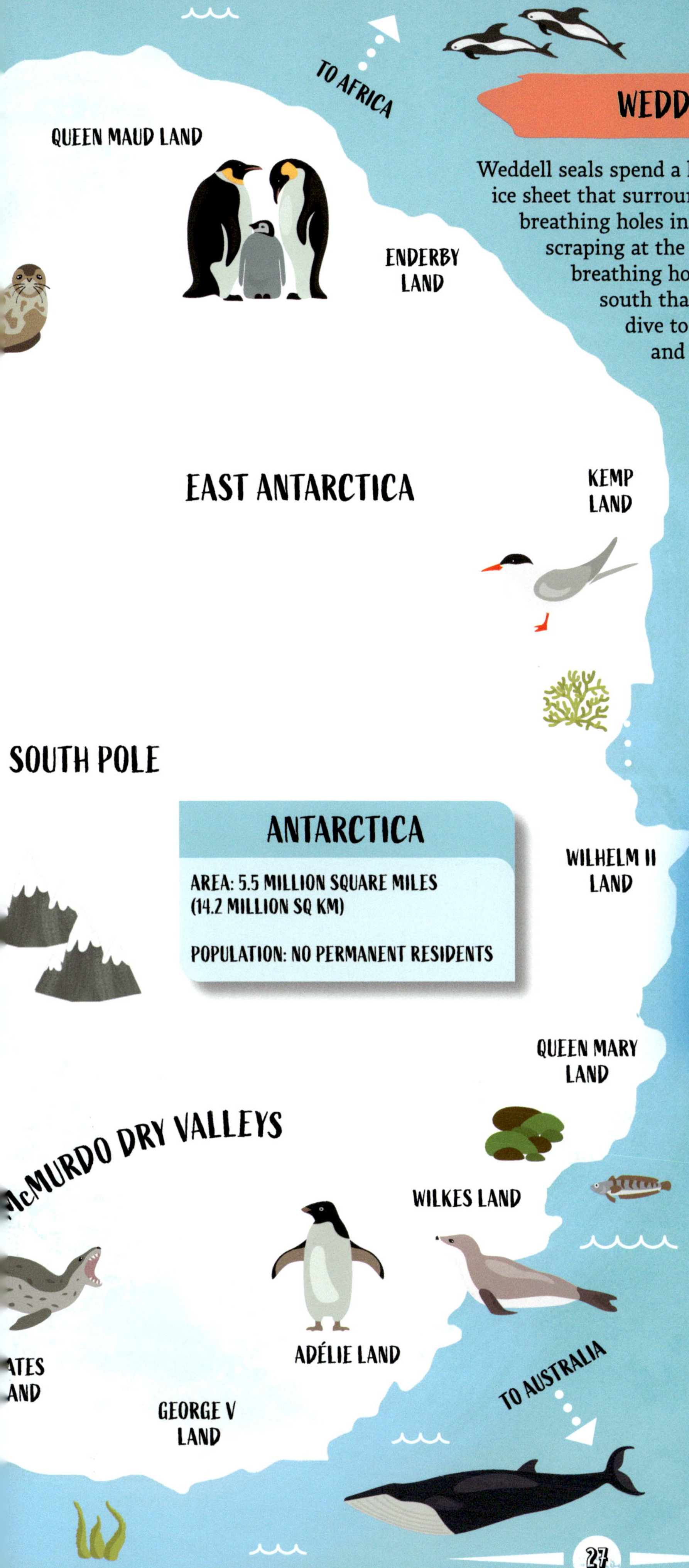

ANTARCTICA

AREA: 5.5 MILLION SQUARE MILES (14.2 MILLION SQ KM)

POPULATION: NO PERMANENT RESIDENTS

WEDDELL SEALS

Weddell seals spend a lot of time feeding under the ice sheet that surrounds Antarctica. The seals make breathing holes in the ice, which they keep open by scraping at the ice with their sharp teeth. These breathing holes allow the seals to live farther south than any other mammal. They can dive to depths of up to 1,968 feet (600 m) and hold their breath for over an hour.

EMPEROR PENGUINS

Standing up to 3 feet (1 m) tall, emperor penguins are the largest species of penguin. The females lay a single egg, then leave the males on the sea ice for two months to incubate the eggs. The males huddle together to keep warm with the eggs held above the ice by their feet. When the females come back, the males can return to the ocean to feed. By this time, they have not eaten anything for four months.

ANTARCTIC PENINSULA

The Antarctic Peninsula is the least-cold part of Antarctica, and a few hardy life-forms survive there, including the continent's only flowering plants. Most of the animals that live on the peninsula catch their food in the ocean, which is rich with small shrimp-like creatures called krill.

FACTS

- Two small flowering plants grow on the open rocks of Antarctica — the Antarctic pearlwort and the Antarctic hair grass. These plants grow only a couple of inches tall but they are the biggest plants on the continent!

- The southern elephant seal is the largest seal in the world. Adult males can grow up to 20 feet (6 m) long and weigh 4 tons — as heavy as a large 4×4 vehicle!

GLOBAL WANDERER

The arctic tern travels farther than any other animal. It spends the northern summer near the North Pole, then flies around the world to spend the southern summer around Antarctica. An arctic tern will fly up to 37,200 miles (60,000 km) in one year. By the end of their lifetimes, they will have traveled a distance equivalent to flying to the moon and back three times!

ACTIVITY

Icebergs

Large icebergs regularly break off the Antarctic Ice Sheet. Ice is less dense than water, which is why the icebergs float, but 90 percent of the ice is underwater. Make your own iceberg to see this in action.

1. With the help of an adult, fill a balloon with water, tie it, and leave it in the freezer overnight. Once it is frozen, take it out and peel away the balloon.

2. Fill a large bowl with water and put your iceberg into the bowl. How much of the ice is sticking out of the top?

QUIZ

1. What is the name of the large sandstone rock in central Australia?

2. Which egg-laying mammal is found in the forests of New Guinea?

3. Which flightless bird is a national symbol of New Zealand?

4. What is the name of the volcano that covers half of the land mass of the island of Hawaii?

5. Which large, hard-shelled fruits were carried to the South Pacific by early human settlers?

6. What is the name of the largest island in French Polynesia?

7. The island of New Guinea is shared by which two countries?

8. What is the Māori name for New Zealand?

9. What is the name of the capital city of Australia?

10. Stone statues called *moai* are found on which Pacific island?

11. How deep can Weddell seals dive for food?

12. Weighing up to 4 tons, what is the name of the largest seal in the world?

Answers:
1. Uluru **2.** Echidna **3.** Kiwi **4.** Mauna Loa **5.** Coconuts **6.** Tahiti
7. Indonesia and Papua New Guinea **8.** Aotearoa **9.** Canberra
10. Easter Island **11.** 1,968 feet (600 m) **12.** Southern elephant seal

GLOSSARY

Ancestor
A person from whom you are descended or were born after.

Archipelago
An area of the ocean containing a large group or chain of small islands.

Coral reef
A stony ridge in the sea formed over time from the skeletons of tiny creatures called coral polyps. An abundance of marine life is found around coral reefs.

Descendants
People who are from later generations.

Dew
Tiny drops of water that form on cool surfaces during the night.

Equator
An imaginary line that divides Earth into the Northern and Southern Hemispheres.

Habitat
An area with the right conditions for a particular set of plants, animals, and other living things to live. Those conditions may include soil type, rainfall, or temperature.

Mammal
A warm-blooded animal with fur or hair on its skin. Female mammals produce milk to feed their young.

Marsupial
A group of mammals whose young are born very underdeveloped and grow inside a pouch in their mother's belly. Marsupials are widespread in Oceania and South America.

Mollusks
A diverse group of animals with soft bodies that live in aquatic or damp habitats. Most mollusks have a hard external shell. Mollusks include snails, mussels, and octopuses.

Photosynthesis
The chemical process by which plants use the energy of the sun to make their food.

Predators
Animals that hunt and kill other animals for food.

Rainforest
A dense forest, rich in life, that grows in areas with plentiful rainfall all year round.

Sandstone
A type of rock formed of sand-sized grains of the mineral quartz.

Scrubland
An area of land with low-growing vegetation, such as small trees and bushes.

Settler
A person who moves to a different country or place to live.

Species
A group of closely related living things that reproduce with one another.

INDEX